OUTLAWS AND LAWMEN
· OF THE WILD WEST ·

BELLE STARR

REVISED EDITION

WANTED
DEAD OR ALIVE

By Carl R. Green and William R. Sanford

Enslow Publishers, Inc.
40 Industrial Road
Box 398
Berkeley Heights, NJ 07922
USA

http://www.enslow.com

Original edition published in 1992.

Library of Congress Cataloging-in-Publication Data
Green, Carl R.
  Belle Starr / Carl R. Green and William R. Sanford.—Rev. ed.
      p. cm. —(Outlaws and lawmen of the wild West)
   Summary: "Learn about Belle Starr, the 'Bandit Queen' of the Wild West. Reader will discover the facts and the legends of this exciting outlaw"—Provided by publisher.
   Includes bibliographical references and index.
   ISBN 978-0-7660-3176-0
  1. Starr, Belle, 1848–1889—Juvenile literature. 2. Women outlaws—West (U.S.)—Biography—Juvenile literature. 3. Outlaws—West (U.S.)—Biography—Juvenile literature. 4. West (U.S.)—Biography—Juvenile literature. 5. Frontier and pioneer life—West (U.S.)—Juvenile literature. I. Sanford, William R. (William Reynolds), 1927– II. Title.
   F594.S8G743 2009
   978'.02092—dc22
   [B]
                                        2008010005

ISBN-10: 0-7660-3176-4

Printed in the United States of America

10 9 8 7 6 5 4 3 2 1

To Our Readers:
We have done our best to make sure all Internet Addresses in this book were active and appropriate when we went to press. However, the authors and the publisher have no control over and assume no liability for the material available on those Internet sites or on other Web sites they may link to. Any comments or suggestions can be sent by e-mail to comments@enslow.com or to the address on the back cover.

♲ Enslow Publishers, Inc., is committed to printing our books on recycled paper. The paper in every book contains 10% to 30% post-consumer waste (PCW). The cover board on the outside of each book contains 100% PCW. Our goal is to do our part to help young people and the environment too!

Interior photos: Alamy/Jill Stephenson, p. 16; Alamy/Paris Pierce, p. 19; The Bridgeman Art Library/Dallas Historical Society, Texas, USA, p. 7; The Bridgeman Art Library/ Private Collection, Peter Newark Western Americana, p. 26; Courtesy Anna M. Bonneman, daughter/Alvin Lederer Collection, pp. 23, 29, 38, 41; Courtesy whitsett-wall.com/Ron Wall, pp. 24, 30, 36, 42; Getty Images, p. 1; The Granger Collection, New York, pp.10, 25; iStockphoto/spxChrome, (marshal badge), odd pages; iStockphoto/Alex Bramwell (revolver), even pages; iStockphoto/ billnoll (frame), pp. 4, 11, 20, 36; The Kobal Collection, p. 44; Legends of America, pp. 5, 6, 11, 13, 17, 20, 27, 33; Public domain, p. 34; Shutterstock/ Dhoxax (background), pp. 3, 5, 8–9, 15, 22–23, 29, 36–37, 43.

Cover photo: Getty Images (*Belle Starr was in her early twenties when this portrait was made. She was married to the outlaw Jim Reed and living high on stolen money.*)

TABLE OF CONTENTS

··· A U T H O R S' N O T E ···

This book tells the true story of the outlaw
Belle Starr. During her lifetime, Belle was
sometimes known as the Bandit Queen. It
was only after she died a violent death that
she became truly famous. That was when
newspapers and magazines began to print
colorful stories about her life and times.
Some of the stories were pure fiction, but
many were true. To the best of the authors'
knowledge, all of the events described in this
book are based on firsthand reports.

CHAPTER ONE

DALLAS LOVED ITS BANDIT QUEEN

Dallas, Texas, was a boomtown in 1874. It was a railroad center, and money flowed freely. Cattle herds that once had to be driven up the long trail to Kansas now moved by rail. The town was proud of its eighteen brick stores and its four banks. It also boasted that Belle Starr, the "Bandit Queen," lived there.

With husband Jim Reed on the run from the law, Belle lived well in Dallas. Stolen money

Belle Starr was well-known in Dallas. She liked fine clothes and always carried her trusty pistol.

Belle always considered herself a lady. She rode sidesaddle to prove it.

paid for her rooms in a good hotel. A maid took care of her children, and a groom cared for her horse.

Belle often rode sidesaddle to prove that she was a lady. She also put on a style show when she went riding. Belle made a handsome figure in her tight black jacket and flowing velvet skirt. Her leather boots gleamed with the same high polish as her saddle. A cowboy hat topped with an ostrich feather shaded her eyes. To complete her outfit she buckled on a gun belt and two loaded pistols.

Dallas was a wide-open town, and Belle liked it that way. She spent much of her time in saloons. When Belle went out on the town, she put on a leather dress trimmed with beads. A necklace of rattlesnake rattles adorned her neck. Like any rowdy cowboy, she drank whiskey and gambled at dice and cards. When the mood hit, she would jump on her horse and gallop through the streets. As she rode, she hollered and fired her pistols in the air.

No one tried to put a stop to Belle's wild rides. It would have been risky to do so. Her husband was a wanted man and some of her best friends were gunslingers. Besides, who cared? Dallas was proud of its spirited Bandit Queen.

Dallas, Texas, was a boomtown in the 1870s, when this map was made. That is also when Belle called it home.

GROWING UP IN MISSOURI

Belle Starr was born February 5, 1848, on a farm in southwest Missouri. Her parents were John and Elizabeth Shirley. At birth, they named the baby Myra Maybelle Shirley. The family called her May. It was years later that May began calling herself Belle. She took the name Starr from her second husband.

In 1851, John Shirley sold his farm for a good price. With money in his pocket, he moved his family to the nearby town of Carthage. There he built the Carthage Hotel, a stable, and a blacksmith shop. His buildings soon took up most of one side of the town square. The Shirley family grew almost as fast as the business. May was the Shirley family's fourth child, after two boys and a girl. In Carthage, Elizabeth gave birth to three more boys.

May had a happy childhood. By the standards of the time, her father was a rich man. That gave her status in Carthage. As a girl, she was small, dark-haired, and pretty. She also had a hot temper. Her friends knew she was ready to fight anyone who annoyed her.

Elizabeth had high hopes for May. She sent her to the Carthage Female Academy to learn to be a lady. May proved to be a good student. She studied languages and music as well as reading, writing, and arithmetic. In the evening, she showed off by playing the piano at the local hotel. The guests spoiled her with their applause and generous gifts.

May's best friend was her older brother Bud. She shared his love of horses and firearms. By the time May was ten, she was a fine rider. Brother and sister spent happy hours riding through the Jasper County hills. Bud also taught May how to handle firearms. She soon became an expert shot with both pistol and rifle.

The Shirleys' peaceful life ended in the late 1850s. The problem of slavery was turning state against state and friend against friend. Missouri was a slave state, and John Shirley was one of the people who owned slaves. The free state of Kansas, however, lay just a few miles away. Both sides were soon sending raiders across the border to steal horses and burn towns.

In 1861, the slave states formed the Confederate States of America. When they tried to leave the Union, the North mobilized to stop them. Men from Jasper County took up arms and joined the Confederate army. Missouri became a Civil War battleground.

In July 1861, Union troops won a victory near Carthage. The rebel army was forced to leave the state, but the fighting raged on. Loyal Southerners

In the late 1850s, violence broke out between the free state of Kansas and the slave state of Missouri. Guerrilla bands on both sides raided towns and farms.

joined guerrilla bands. The bands ambushed Union troops and tore up rail lines. To John Shirley, the guerrillas were all heroes. Bud shared his father's feelings. He joined Quantrill's Raiders, a band led by William C. Quantrill.

May was only fourteen years old, but she wanted to help. She could not join the raiders, so she became

During the Civil War, William Quantrill led one of the most well-known rebel guerrilla bands.

a spy. Her job was to keep track of the Union forces. How many men did they have? Where were they camped? What kind of guns did they carry? She gathered the information and passed it on to the rebels.

Quantrill now led over a thousand men. Young Jim Reed was one of the newest Raiders. Jim, also from Carthage, was May's sweetheart. In August 1862, the Raiders cut railroad lines and won a few small battles. The Union forces struck back, forcing the

Raiders to fight for their lives. By December things were too hot for Quantrill. He broke off the action and led his men into Arkansas.

Two months later, May made a brave ride to save her brother. Some writers say there is no proof that the ride took place. Others are certain it did. Here is the story.

Early in the New Year, Bud came home on leave. While he was in Carthage, May went on a scouting trip. Her ride took her to Newtonia, thirty-five miles away. Major Eno of the Union cavalry had his command post there. To her dismay, May learned that Eno had sent soldiers to arrest Bud. She wanted to ride home to warn him, but she was captured before she could saddle up. When he saw her, Eno took a fancy to the pretty young rebel. He took her to the house he used as a headquarters and guarded her himself.

May was not afraid of him. She stamped her foot and swore at the major. When Eno laughed at her, she became even angrier. She sat down at the piano and pounded out one loud tune after another. After putting up with her for a time, Eno let May go. He was sure she could not beat his men to Carthage.

That was a mistake. May cut across the countryside. With reckless courage, she jumped fences

Some say there is no proof that Belle made a daring ride to save her brother Bud in 1863. Belle's fans love the story anyway.

and streams. When her horse slowed, she lashed it with a whip. Thanks to her wild ride, May was waiting when Eno's men rode into town. She smiled and greeted the dusty soldiers. "Captain Shirley isn't here," she told them. "He left half an hour ago."

Bud could not escape the next Union trap. In June 1864, a troop of Union soldiers moved into Carthage. They soon learned that Bud and a friend were staying at a house in a nearby town. Moving quickly, they surrounded the house. Bud was shot and killed as he tried to escape by jumping over a fence.

May swore to avenge Bud's death, but there was little she could do. The war was coming to a close. With his son dead, a saddened John Shirley said he was sick of fighting. He sold his properties and loaded the family into two covered wagons. May did not want to leave Jim Reed, but she obeyed her father. She drove one of the wagons as the family headed toward Texas. Preston, her older brother, already had a farm near Dallas.

CHAPTER THREE

MARRYING AN OUTLAW

The Shirleys were not the only ones moving. Many of the houses in Carthage stood vacant, marked with the letters G.T.T. Everyone knew the letters stood for *Gone to Texas*.

Dallas was still a small town when May first saw it. Wooden sidewalks lined streets that turned into muddy streams when it rained. Farmers and cowboys bought supplies and looked for fun on Main Street. General stores sold a wide array of goods. Gambling halls and saloons promised a good time.

John Shirley settled in Scyene, southeast of Dallas. He claimed some land above South Mesquite Creek. The fertile black soil was good for growing corn and other crops. Shirley also raised hogs and fast horses. At first, the family lived in a cabin. Later, Shirley moved them into a four-room house, the largest in Scyene. When the creek ran dry, May filled barrels of water at

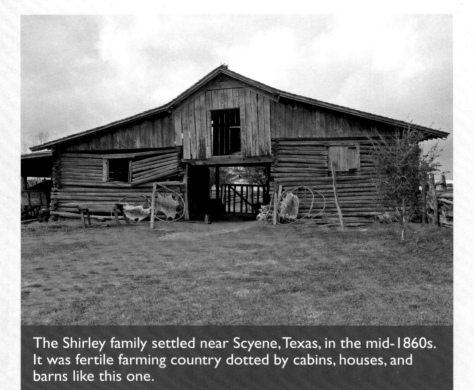

The Shirley family settled near Scyene, Texas, in the mid-1860s. It was fertile farming country dotted by cabins, houses, and barns like this one.

the town well. Then she dragged the heavy barrels home on a sled.

By Texas standards May was well-educated. Proud of her book learning, she looked down on the town's one-room school. Instead of going to class, she kept busy at home. She cared for her younger brothers and tended the garden. For fun she rode her horse along Mesquite Creek. When May stopped to gossip, she asked for the latest news from Missouri. A traveler most likely told her about Jesse James and his gang.

In 1866, the James gang robbed a bank of cash and gold coins. Then the outlaws rode to San Antonio, Texas, to swap the gold for paper money. Far from Missouri, banks in San Antonio did not ask questions about the source of the coins. On the way back to Missouri, the gang stopped at John Shirley's house. He was glad to see Jesse and the four Younger brothers—Jim, Cole, Bob, and John. Shirley was a law-abiding man, but the Youngers were old friends from Missouri.

Some writers argue that a romance blossomed during the visit. They claim that Cole Younger was the father of May's first child. Cole probably did admire May's good looks. Many men did. But Cole always denied that he was May's lover. More to the point, May's daughter was not born until two years later.

Bob, Jim, and Cole Younger (left to right), along with their brother John, were all members of Jesse James's gang. They are pictured with their sister Henrietta. Belle's family also counted them as friends.

Jim Reed was the man who made May's heart beat faster. Jim and his family had followed the Shirleys to Texas. May was happy to see her old sweetheart again. After the reunion, the courtship moved swiftly. On November 1, 1866, Jim and May were married.

Did John Shirley try to keep the lovers apart? Some accounts claim that he did not want May to marry Jim Reed. As they tell the story, Jim and his friends carried May off on horseback. Once safely away, they stopped for a hasty wedding—still on horseback.

The elopement makes a good story, but the facts do not back it up. The Reeds and the Shirleys were good friends. After the wedding, Jim and May moved in with her parents. Jim helped his father-in-law raise hogs and horses.

A year later, Jim's mother moved back to Missouri. The young couple went with her. Jim worked the family farm at Rich Hill. There, in 1868, May gave birth to a daughter. She named the baby Rosie Lee, but always spoke of her as "my pearl." Soon everyone was calling the baby Pearl.

May was happy enough, but Jim was bored with farm life. He gambled, raced horses, and spent time in the Indian Territory. While there, he made friends with Tom Starr, a member of the Cherokee

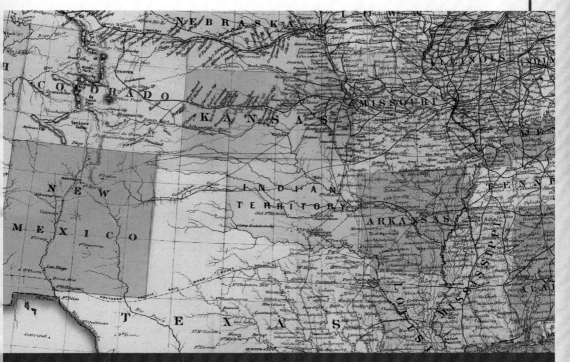

A map of the United States from 1872 shows Indian Territory
(to the north of Texas), which later became the state of Oklahoma.
Belle and Jim lived in southwestern Missouri, a short distance away.

tribe. Starr was the head of a large family that had little respect for the law.

Trouble seemed to follow Jim Reed. After his brother was murdered, Jim chased the killers into Arkansas and shot them. The killings left him saddled with a murder charge of his own. Jim picked up May and Pearl and sought safety with Tom Starr. Arkansas lawmen could not arrest him on Indian land.

Restless and fearful, Jim moved his family to the West Coast. It was around this time that May began to call herself Belle. In 1871, she gave birth to a son in Los Angeles, California. She named the baby James Edward. Life was good until Jim was arrested for passing fake money. To make matters worse, the police then learned that he was wanted for murder in Arkansas. Jim soon jumped bail and headed east. Belle, Pearl, and little Eddie followed by stagecoach.

Belle's husband Jim Reed was an outlaw in his own right. He spent much of their marriage on the run from the law.

Back in Texas, Belle's father gave the Reeds a farm to work. Jim and Belle turned it into a hideout for horse thieves. But Jim still had a price on his head. Leaving the children in Scyene with her family, he and Belle headed north to the Indian Territory. There, in the fall of 1873, Jim and some friends tortured and robbed a rich farmer. They escaped with $30,000.

Three months later, the law came looking for Jim. He went into hiding, and Belle moved back to her parents' house. For excitement, she lived part-time in a Dallas hotel. That was when people began to call her the Bandit Queen. Belle did not mind. She was having a good time spending Jim's stolen money.

The marriage broke up in 1874. Jim had acquired a new girlfriend and a new gang. On April 7 the Reed gang held up the Austin stage. The gunmen robbed the passengers and plundered the mail sacks. At the time, stagecoach holdups were new to Texas. A large reward was posted for the capture of the gang.

A lawman named John Morris tracked Jim to Paris, Texas. Morris wanted the reward, but he did not want to risk a gunfight. Posing as a friend, Morris talked Jim into a plan to rob an old man. On the way, they stopped to rest at an inn. Morris pulled his gun while Jim was eating lunch. Jim, who was unarmed, picked up a table and ran toward the lawman. Morris fired. The bullets smashed through the table and hit the outlaw in the chest.

The killing earned Morris a reward of $1,700. It also left Belle a widow.

BELLE FALLS IN WITH MORE BAD COMPANY

Little is known of Belle's life in the four years after Jim Reed's death. It is clear that she did not fulfill her mother's hopes that she would become a lady. Although she still dressed well, she looked old for her years. Her hands were roughened by the hard work of farming and keeping house. Her skin was burned by the summer sun and chapped by the winter cold. She spent more time with outlaws than with honest folk.

John Shirley died in 1876. Belle, who was living near Dallas, sold the farm he had given her. She paid for Pearl to go to acting school. Eddie was more of a problem. She loved her son, but the two fought all the time. At last, Belle sent him to Missouri to live with his Grammy Reed at Rich Hill.

Belle liked men, and men liked her. For a while, she was seen with a Kansas miner named Bruce Younger. Bruce was an uncle of the Younger brothers, and an old family friend. Another time a rich rancher came to her aid. Belle had been put on trial for burning a store. The rancher saw her in court and liked what he saw. After helping her win the case, he gave Belle a large sum of money.

When Belle married again she chose Tom Starr's son Sam. She liked big men and Sam Starr stood six feet, five inches tall. The handsome Cherokee was also nine years younger than Belle. In 1880, the two joined hands in a tribal wedding.

Belle and Sam claimed a thousand acres of Indian

Belle's second husband was the tall, handsome Sam Starr. They married in 1880.

After they married, Belle and Sam Starr claimed some land on the Canadian River in Indian Territory. Belle called their farm Younger's Bend.

land on the Canadian River. Their farm, with its typical frontier house, was forty miles west of Fort Smith, Arkansas. Their first house had one room and a lean-to kitchen in back. A sagging front porch shaded the front of the house. Water came from a nearby spring. Belle did her best to decorate her crude home. She bought a bolt of flower-print fabric and used it to cover the walls.

When Belle was settled, Pearl came to live with her. The girl was a big help around the house and in the garden. Belle called her farm Younger's Bend.

She wrote: "On the Canadian River . . . I hoped to pass the remainder of my life in peace."

That hope soon died. Most of Sam and Belle's friends were outlaws. Younger's Bend became a hideout. The only way into the farm was through a brush-filled canyon. Lookouts kept watch, ready to sound the alarm if a lawman came their way. The outlaws also hid in Robber's Cave, which was a day's ride away. Today, the cave is a popular tourist spot.

Belle claimed that Jesse James was her first "guest." In time, business was so good she had to build two more cabins. The outlaws stayed busy while they were at Younger's Bend. They stole horses, robbed salesmen, and sold moonshine whiskey to

Many outlaws stayed at Younger's Bend. Jesse James (above) was a welcome visitor.

the Indians. Belle sat in on meetings and helped plan new crimes. She also bought and sold stolen horses.

REWARD

$10,000

IN GOLD COIN

Will be paid by the U. S. Government for the apprehension

DEAD OR ALIVE

of

SAM and BELLE STARR

Wanted for Robbery, Murder, Treason and other acts against the peace and dignity of the U. S.

THOMAS CRAIL

Major, 8th Missouri Cavalry, Commanding

Fake reward posters like this are part of Belle's myth. The Starrs were never guilty of murder or treason. Only famous outlaws like Jesse James commanded such huge rewards.

In 1882, Belle's dealings in horses brought the law to Younger's Bend. A U.S. Marshal charged that she and Sam had stolen a horse. The horse's owner, Andrew Crane, had valued the horse at eighty dollars. The marshal arrested Belle and Sam and took them to jail in Fort Smith.

Belle was no stranger to jails. One story claims that she was first jailed in 1878. If the story is true, Belle so charmed her jailer that he set her free. When she fled, he rode off with her. A few days later, the story goes, she tied the jailer to his horse and sent him back. Pinned to his badge was a note that said he was "unsatisfactory."

At Fort Smith, a hearing was held on the horse-stealing charge. Andrew Crane testified that Belle told him a man named Childs took the horse.

A neighbor, however, swore he had seen Belle riding Crane's horse. That was enough for the court. Belle and Sam were ordered to stand trial. They went free on bail after Tom Starr put up the bail money. Belle hired a lawyer to defend them.

The four-day trial took place in 1883. Sam claimed that he was sick with measles at the time of the theft. No one, however, could pin down the date when the measles epidemic broke out. Belle stuck to her story that Childs had the horse, but Childs had gone off to Texas. When the case went to the jury, both Starrs were found guilty.

Belle and Sam had good reason to fear a long jail term. Judge Isaac Parker was due to pass sentence on them. Judge Parker was better known as the Hanging Judge. In all, he sent eighty-eight men to die on the gallows.

For once, Parker showed mercy. He could have sent the Starrs to prison for many years.

Judge Isaac Parker had a reputation as a "Hanging Judge," but he went easy on Belle and Sam.

Instead, he gave them one-year terms in a Michigan prison. If they stayed out of trouble they could be out in nine months. Many stories are told of Belle spending time in one jail or another. Her stay in Michigan, however, is the only jail term for which records exist.

In Michigan, Belle and Sam had a second stroke of luck. The prison they were sent to tried to help its inmates reform. Belle was put to work weaving cane bottoms for chairs, but she soon caught the warden's eye. He put her to work in his office and let her teach music to his children. In her spare time, Belle began writing a love story. Sam's life was harder. He spent the long days breaking rocks with a sledgehammer.

The Starrs were set free at the end of nine months. Belle was anxious to return to Younger's Bend. There were crops to plant and a house to care for. Most of all, she missed her children, who had been staying with trusted friends. Before going to prison she had written to Pearl to describe their future. In the letter she said, "We will have Eddie with us and will be as gay and happy as the birds. . . ."

BELLE TURNS OVER A NEW LEAF

With their prison term ended, Belle and Sam headed home. On the way, they picked up Pearl and Mabel Harrison. Mabel was an orphan who had become Pearl's best friend. Back at Younger's Bend, Belle fixed up the house. Sam planted the spring crops.

Belle did not like to cook, so the girls fixed the meals. For special days, Belle sometimes whipped up a batch of sugar candy. The day Eddie came home was one of those occasions. For the first time in years, Belle had both children with her. The day a piano arrived

After her time in prison, Belle went back to Younger's Bend with Sam. But their quiet home life did not last long.

29

at Younger's Bend was equally special. Belle happily banged out church hymns and songs such as "Listen to the Mockingbird." Pearl and Eddie took lessons, but neither showed much musical talent.

Belle's son, Eddie, came to live with his mother at Younger's Bend when he was in his early teens. This picture was taken when Eddie was in his twenties.

The peaceful times ended all too soon. In 1885, Sam was accused of robbing a store and post office. With the law on his trail, he went into hiding. Indian police often came to Younger's Bend to look for him. Only when the coast was clear could Sam visit Belle and the children.

Belle was having troubles of her own. Three months after Sam left she again was accused of stealing horses. Belle went to Fort Smith and entered a not-guilty plea. While she was free on bail, she also was charged with taking part in a robbery. The judge dismissed those charges.

In the fall, Belle was tried on the horse-stealing charge. She produced a witness who swore that Belle had paid a stranger fifty dollars for the horse. The jury believed the witness and found her not guilty. Even so, Belle could not relax. Word had reached her that Sam had been shot.

Feeling safe for the moment, Sam had gone riding on Venus, Belle's best horse. As luck would have it, he ran into a four-man posse. Frank West, an old enemy, opened fire without warning. One bullet killed Venus and another grazed Sam's head. Luckily for Sam, the bloody wound looked worse than it was. After two of the men left to find a wagon, Sam grabbed a rifle and disarmed his guards. Then he escaped on one of their horses.

Belle nursed Sam at his brother's house. As he healed, she argued that he should give himself up. She told Sam the Indian police would kill him if they found him. Sam saw that she had a point. He surrendered to a lawman who took him to Fort Smith. Belle rode behind the two men, twin pistols strapped to her waist. After Sam was charged, she put up his bail.

All was calm until a week before Christmas. The Starrs went to a dance at a neighbor's house. Belle played the organ for the dancing. During the party, someone ran in to warn Sam that Frank West was outside. Sam confronted West and accused him of killing Venus. In the next instant, the two men were reaching for their guns. Sam fired first; West, an instant later. When the smoke cleared, both men were dead.

Belle cradled Sam's head in her lap and cursed Frank West. She had loved her outlaw husband. Sam's death, moreover, meant that she could not keep her farm. Only Cherokees could live on Cherokee land. Belle would have to move unless she married another Cherokee.

Finding a new man was never a big problem for Belle. Some stories claim she had been seeing other men the whole time. John Middleton may have been one of her lovers. Gossip says that Belle was ready to run off with him. If so, Sam had spoiled the plan by showing up before they could leave. No one knows what happened next. The only certainty is that Middleton's body was found a few days later.

Other stories say Belle loved an Indian outlaw named Blue Duck. Blue Duck, it seems, lost all of his money in a gambling hall. Belle showed up there the next night. Pistol in hand, she took back the money Blue Duck had lost. As she left, someone accused her of taking too much. "Come to my farm and get it," she yelled back. No one took her up on the offer.

A photo of Belle and Blue Duck does exist. Experts say she posed at the request of friends.

No one knows for sure if Belle was in love with Indian outlaw Blue Duck (left). Experts say she posed with him as a favor.

Being seen with her, they thought, might help Blue Duck. At the time, he was on trial for murder.

In early 1887, Belle invited Tom Starr's adopted son to move in with her. At twenty-four, Jim July Starr was fifteen years younger than Belle. With July by her side, Belle could keep her farm. She also turned over a new leaf. Belle put out the word that outlaws were no longer welcome at Younger's Bend.

Pearl was now a headstrong nineteen and quick to argue with her mother. Jim July was a frequent target of her anger. Belle objected when Pearl called Jim a lazy horse thief. It was Pearl's boyfriends, however, who caused the most trouble. One young man had gone so far as to ask for Pearl's hand in marriage. Belle turned him down. She did not want her daughter to marry a poor man. That was too much for Pearl. She left home and went to live with her grandmother in Arkansas. That fall, she gave birth to a daughter she named Flossie.

Belle's daughter Pearl (right) was close to her mother, but they often argued. Pearl left home when she was nineteen and soon gave birth to a daughter of her own.

Pearl was only one of Belle's worries. After Jim July was jailed for stealing a horse, Belle refused to help him.

When he got out on bail, she gave him a public scolding. Young Eddie was also in and out of trouble. In the summer of 1888, he and Mose Perryman got into a fight over a stolen horse. Mose ended the dispute by shooting Eddie in the head.

Belle brought her wounded son back to the farm. When Pearl heard about the shooting, she came home to nurse her brother. As Eddie's wound healed, his arguments with Belle heated up. After one quarrel, Belle ordered the village postmaster not to give Eddie her mail. Eddie did not take the insult lying down. He drew his pistol and took his mother's letters at gunpoint.

When Belle heard about the stolen letters, she lashed Eddie with her whip. Later, she whipped him again when he abused her horse. That was too much for Eddie. He moved out. Belle never saw him again.

THE DEATH OF THE BANDIT QUEEN

Belle turned forty in 1888. She looked older. Hard living had streaked her black hair with gray. Her skin was burned by sun and wind to a leathery brown. Her nose stuck out as sharp as an eagle's beak. People whispered that she looked like an Indian.

Even so, men turned to stare when Belle rode by. Proud of her small feet, she wore only the finest boots. When riding, she always carried "my baby." "Baby" was a Colt .45 pistol.

By the time she was in her early forties, Belle had lost two husbands. Hard living had taken its toll on her.

Belle held fast to what was left of her ladylike ways. A shelf in her cabin held her father's books. She played the piano and organ. Some women smoked cigars when they gambled in the saloons. Belle liked to gamble, but she never lit up a cigar.

One day, as she was riding near Fort Smith, her hat blew off. A cowboy saw the hat flutter by, but refused to chase it. Belle drew her Colt and ordered him to pick it up. The surprised cowboy did as he was told. Belle took the hat and put it on. Then she said, "The next time a lady asks you to pick up her hat, do as she tells you!"

This was the "new" Belle. Outlaws were not allowed to stay at her farm. Her neighbors no longer lost their stock to her "guests." When friends came by, Belle showed them a letter from Robert Owen, the local Indian Agent. Owen had written to say that a complaint against Belle had been dropped. He praised her for keeping "bad characters" away from Younger's Bend.

If Belle was changing, so was the Indian Territory. The Indians now were renting rich bottom land to settlers. Poor farmers from the South jumped at the offer. They paid a rent of one-fourth of the cotton and corn they raised.

Like her neighbors, Belle rented parcels of her own land. One of the would-be tenants was Edgar Watson. Watson knew the fertile black soil would grow good crops. Also, as Belle's tenant, he would not have to take out a new lease each year.

The deal went sour when Belle became friends with Watson's wife. Mrs. Watson told Belle about her husband's past. She said that Watson was wanted on a Florida murder charge. That upset Belle. She had befriended dozens of bad men in her day. But now she was trying to go straight.

Edgar Watson planned to rent land from Belle. When she found out about his murderous past, she refused to make the deal. It was a fatal move.

Belle offered to return Watson's rent money. Watson refused to take it. Next, Belle sent the money back in a letter. She also wrote that someone else was taking over the Watson farm. Watson proved to be just as stubborn. He scared the new tenant into backing out of the deal.

That was enough for Belle. She warned Watson that she knew his secret and ordered him to clear out. Watson did not argue with her. When she was done, he climbed on his horse and rode away. Pearl watched him leave and urged her mother to be careful. Belle only laughed.

On February 2, 1889, Jim July saddled up to ride to Fort Smith. He was due there to face the old horse-stealing charge. Belle rode the ten miles to King Creek with him. She had a bill to pay at the store there. Later, the two rode on to spend the night with friends. In the morning, Jim went on to Fort Smith. Belle headed back to her farm.

By midday she was eating lunch at King Creek. The storeowner asked her why she looked so gloomy. Belle said she feared that someone would try to kill her.

Belle's next stop was at Jackson Rowe's house. She did not see Edgar Watson leave the house as she came up the road. When she reached the porch, Belle stopped to chat. After eating a piece of corn bread, she asked about her son. Eddie was living with the Rowes, but he had gone off to see a friend.

When Belle left, she turned into the muddy lane that led to the river. She did not see the figure hiding behind a fence. Belle was only twenty feet away when the man fired a shotgun. Buckshot tore into her back and neck. She fell from her horse and splashed into the mud. As she tried to rise, the killer ran up and fired again.

Down by the river a neighbor saw Belle's horse dash by. He raced up the road and found her lying in a pool of blood. By the time he brought Pearl to the spot, Belle Starr was dead.

The funeral was held three days later. Neighbor women dressed Belle in her best riding clothes. As a final touch, Pearl placed her mother's pistol in her hand. Some Indian friends lowered the pine coffin into a grave near the river.

After the grave was closed, Jim July pulled a gun. He accused Watson of killing Belle. A court hearing was held, but there was no proof that Watson was the killer. Guilty or not, Watson packed up and left. He knew July would kill him if he stayed.

United States of America,

Western District of Arkansas.

The President of the United States of America,

To the Marshal for the Western District of Arkansas, and the Keeper of the United States Jail----Greeting :

WHEREAS *Edgar A. Watson*

has been arrested and this day brought before STEPHEN WHEELER, a Commissioner appointed by the

District Court of the United States, in and for the Western District of Arkansas, under the laws of the United

States, charged on the oath of *J. L. Starr* with

Murder in the Indian Country

and, there not being sufficient time to hear and decide upon the charge against *him*

on this day *he* was required to give

bail in a sufficient sum for his appearance before me on such day as the charge against him can be heard and

decided upon, which requisition he has failed to comply with.

WE THEREFORE COMMAND YOU, the said Marshal, forthwith to convey the said

Edgar A. Watson to the United States Jail at Fort Smith,

and *him* deliver to the Keeper thereof. And you, the said Keeper, are hereby required to re-

ceive the said *Edgar A. Watson*

into your custody in the said jail, and *him* there safely keep until *he* shall be

discharged by due course of law.

GIVEN under my hand, this *8th* day of *February*

A. D. 188*9*, in the 113th year of our Independence.

Stephen Wheeler

Commissioner U. S. Court, Western District of Arkansas.

After Belle's death in 1889, an arrest warrant was issued for Edgar Watson. Despite this, no one could prove he was the killer.

Despite their frequent arguments, Pearl loved her mother. She ordered a tombstone for Belle's grave. The poem she chose to have carved on the stone reads:

Shed not for her the bitter tear,
Nor give the heart to vain regret;
'Tis but the casket that lies here,
The gem that filled it sparkles yet.

Belle was buried near the Canadian River in her best riding clothes, with her pistol in her hand.

THE LEGEND OF THE BANDIT QUEEN

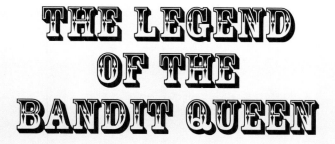

Newspapers splashed the murder of Belle Starr across their front pages. All across the country, readers snapped up the papers. They wanted to learn about the Bandit Queen. The report in *The New York Times* said Belle was . . .

> . . . *the most desperate woman that ever figured on the borders. She married Cole Younger . . . but left him and joined a band of outlaws that operated in the Indian Territory. She had been arrested for murder and robbery a score of times, but always managed to escape.*

The paper spelled her name right. None of the other "facts" were true.

A reporter named Alton Meyers cashed in on Belle's fame. Without checking his facts, he rushed a book into print. It was called *Bella Starr, the Bandit*

Queen, or the *Female Jesse James.* After that, the myths piled up quickly. A few examples:

Myth: Belle Starr rode with Quantrill's Raiders during the Civil War. In fact, only two women rode with Quantrill. Belle was not one of them.

Myth: Belle Starr would just as soon kill a man as look at him. In fact, Belle never killed anyone. She threatened to kill a few, but never pulled the trigger on them.

Myth: Like Jesse James, Belle was the leader of an outlaw gang. In fact, Belle was never part of a gang. She did make money buying and selling stolen horses. She also accepted money from the outlaws who stayed with her.

Today, the myths live on in books, films, and songs. Belle is always billed as the "Bandit Queen." That title may be the biggest myth of all. The lawless Wild West never had a true Bandit Queen. Belle Starr, however, came closer to earning that title than anyone else.

A 1941 movie brought Belle Starr's legend to a whole new generation.

GLOSSARY

bail—Money paid to a court to guarantee the return of a suspect for trial.

Civil War—The war fought between the North (the Union) and the South (the Confederacy), 1861–1865.

gallows—The platform on which a convicted criminal is hanged.

guerrilla bands—Small, fast-moving military units that operate outside the normal rules of warfare.

gunslingers—Outlaws and lawmen of the Wild West who preferred to settle arguments with their pistols.

Hanging Judge—A judge with a reputation for giving death sentences.

Indian Agent—A federal worker who has the job of making sure that the Indians in a particular area are treated fairly.

Indian Territory—An area set aside for Indian tribes forced to leave their own land. The Cherokee territory Belle Starr lived in is now part of Oklahoma.

jury—A group of people sworn to judge the facts and arrive at a decision in a court case.

myth—A story that many people believe, but which is almost always untrue.

posse—A group of citizens who join with law enforcement officers to aid in the capture of outlaws.

Quantrill's Raiders—A band of Southern guerrillas led by William Quantrill. The Raiders fought against Union forces in Missouri.

sidesaddle—A special woman's saddle made with two saddle horns (one lower than the other) and a single stirrup. The design allows women to ride with both legs on the left side of the horse.

stage—Short for stagecoach. A horse-drawn coach that traveled a regular route with passengers or mail.

Union—The name given to the Northern states that fought against the South during the Civil War.

FURTHER READING

Books

Bard, Jessica. *Lawmen and Outlaws: The Wild, Wild West.* Danbury, Conn.: Children's Press, 2005.

Krohn, Katherine E. *Wild West Women.* Minneapolis: Lerner, 2005.

Shackleford, William Yancey. *Belle Starr, the Bandit Queen: The Career of the Most Colorful Outlaw the Indian Territory Ever Knew.* Whitefish, Mont.: Kessinger Publishing, 2007.

Weil, Ann. *Outlaws.* Chicago: Raintree, 2008.

Internet Addresses

HistoryNet.com: Belle Starr
http://www.historynet.com/belle-starr.htm

Women in History: Belle Starr
http://www.lkwdpl.org/wihohio/star-bel.htm

INDEX